Visual Science Encyclopedia

Weather

▲ Fair weather cumulus seen from above. These clouds represent places where warm air is rising, and the air is cooling, condensing, and producing water droplets to form the cloud. The clear areas in between are where air is sinking and warming.

How to use this book

Every word defined in this book can be found in alphabetical order on pages 3 to 47. There is also a full index on page 48. A number of other features will help you get the most out of the *Visual Science Encyclopedia*. They are shown below.

Here you will find the first word defined on any left-hand page.

Here you will find the last word defined on any right-hand page.

Each word is shown in bold so it is easy to find.

Each new letter of the alphabet is clearly marked to help you find the word you are looking for quicker.

Other words defined in the book are highlighted in bold.

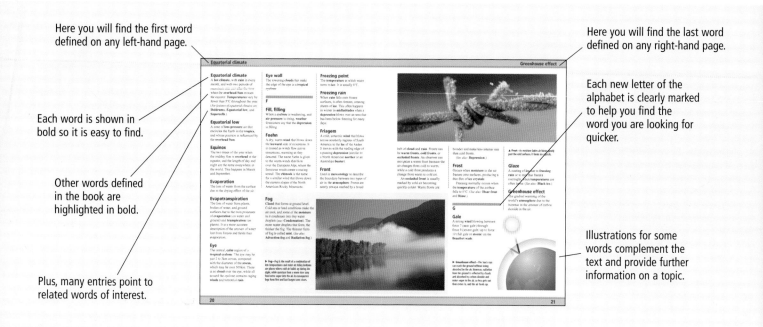

Illustrations for some words complement the text and provide further information on a topic.

Plus, many entries point to related words of interest.

Acknowledgments

Grolier Educational
First published in the United States in 2002 by Grolier Educational, Sherman Turnpike, Danbury, CT 06816

Copyright © 2002
Atlantic Europe Publishing Company Ltd.

All rights reserved. No part of this publication may be reproduced, stored in a retrieval system, or transmitted in any form or by any means—electronic, mechanical, photocopying, recording, or otherwise—without prior permission of the publisher.

Author
Brian Knapp, BSc, PhD

Art Director
Duncan McCrae, BSc

Senior Designer
Adele Humphries, BA, PGCE

Editors
Lisa Magloff, BA, and Mary Sanders, BSc

Illustrations
David Woodroffe

Designed and produced by
EARTHSCAPE EDITIONS

Reproduced in Malaysia by
Global Color

Printed in Hong Kong by
Wing King Tong Company Ltd.

**Library of Congress
Cataloging-in-Publication Data**
Visual Science Encyclopedia
       p. cm.
    Includes indexes.
    Contents: v. 1. Weather—v. 2.
Elements—v. 3. Rocks, minerals, and soil—
v. 4. Forces—v. 5. Light and sound—
v. 6. Water—v. 7. Plants—v. 8. Electricity
and magnetism—v. 9. Earth and space—
v. 10. Computers and the Internet—v. 11.
Earthquakes and volcanoes—v. 12. Heat
and energy.
    ISBN 0-7172-5595-6 (set: alk. paper)—ISBN
0-7172-5596-4 (v. 1: alk. paper)—ISBN
0-7172-5597-2 (v. 2: alk. paper)—ISBN
0-7172-5598-0 (v. 3: alk. paper)—ISBN
0-7172-5599-9 (v. 4: alk. paper)—ISBN
0-7172-5600-6 (v. 5: alk. paper)—ISBN
0-7172-5601-4 (v. 6: alk. paper)—ISBN
0-7172-5602-2 (v. 7: alk. paper)—ISBN
0-7172-5603-0 (v. 8: alk. paper)—ISBN
0-7172-5604-9 (v. 9: alk. paper)—ISBN
0-7172-5605-7 (v. 10: alk. paper)—ISBN
0-7172-5606-5 (v. 11: alk. paper)—ISBN
0-7172-5607-3 (v. 12: alk. paper)
    1. Science—Encyclopedias, Juvenile.
[1. Science—Encyclopedias.] I. Grolier
Educational (Firm)

QI21.V58 2001
503—dc21
                                            2001023704

Picture credits
All photographs are from the Earthscape Editions photolibrary except the following:
(c=center t=top b=bottom l=left r=right)

NASA 9tr, 9bl, 25tl; *Courtesy of the University of Dundee* 16cr; *NOAA* 25tr, 42cr; *ZEFA* 26b.

This product is manufactured from sustainable managed forests. For every tree cut down, at least one more is planted.

A

Acid rain

Rain that has been polluted with acid gases. This form of **pollution** is connected with the release of sulfur and nitrogen gases when fossil fuels are burned, for example, in power stations or by vehicles. The gases combine with water droplets in the **clouds** to form dilute acids and then fall as rain.

Adret

The (morning) sunny side of a mountain valley; the opposite slope is known as the ubac. The adret is important in mountainous areas because the side with the morning Sun warms up and becomes **frost**-free soonest. It is the side of a valley where most houses are built.

Advection

When air flows horizontally from one area to another.

▼ Adret—How the rising Sun warms one side of a valley faster than the other.

Sunny side of the valley. The sunshine warms the houses and fields on this side of the valley first, so it is a far more attractive place to live.

Shady side of the valley

Advection fog

A **fog** produced when warm air flows across a cold ocean. The air is cooled until the **moisture** cannot all be held as vapor, and then some of it **condenses** into droplets, creating fog. Advection fog makes banks of fog. It is not blown away by **wind**, but is often made more dense and widespread. Advection fogs are common in summer off the coast of California, where they are sometimes called Tullee fogs, and off the Grand Banks (Newfoundland) through much of the year.

▼ Advection fog—Dense advection fog partly obscuring the Golden Gate Bridge, San Francisco.

Air mass

A part of the **atmosphere** with the same kind of air that makes a particular kind of **weather**. The air mass is named after the place where the air took on its **temperature** and **humidity**. Some typical air masses are called **arctic air**, **polar air**, tropical maritime air, and polar continental air. An air mass that forms over the tropical oceans will be moist and warm. An **air stream** leaving this kind of air mass will cause hot, sultry, and sometimes thundery weather (often called **dog days** in summer). In contrast, air streaming away from a polar continental air mass in winter will be very cold, but also very dry, and the sky will be cloudless.

Air masses are changed as they move from the places where they formed. For example, polar continental air is dry; but if the air stream leaving it flows over an ocean, it will pick up **moisture** and warmth, and be likely to cause showers of **sleet** and **snow**.

Air pressure

The force per square meter exerted by the air on the ground. An area of **high pressure** is formed where air **currents** make air sink over a region of the Earth; an area of **low pressure** is a region where air is rising and so reducing the typical weight of air at that place. A high-pressure region can also be caused by air flowing into a place faster than it flows out. A low-pressure area can be formed if air flows out faster than it flows in. These effects are commonly a cause of **depressions** in the **midlatitudes**.

Air stream

A flow of similar air, for example, a flow of **westerly winds** across the Atlantic or Pacific.

Albedo

Used in **meteorology** to describe the reflectivity of natural surfaces.

A surface, such as bare rock, has an albedo, or reflectivity, of about 30%, meaning that 70% of the light is absorbed. Oceans can have albedos as high as 90% if the Sun is **overhead** at the **tropics**, but as little as 10% at sunrise or sunset or in polar latitudes. These differences affect the amount of **heat** the Earth is able to absorb from the Sun.

However, the greatest albedo of all is from the top of **clouds** and from snowfields, which often register over 95% albedo.

Aleutian low

A part of the **atmosphere** above the northeast Pacific Ocean that commonly has **low-pressure** air. It is a place where low-pressure systems, or **depressions**, are formed, or where they grow (deepen). It is strongest in winter.

Altitude

The height above sea level. It is measured in meters.

Alto-

Used when describing **clouds**, meaning medium height.

Altocumulus

A word used for **cumulus clouds** of medium height. They are thin **clouds** and normally look white. They form as a result of upward movement of the air. Sometimes this is a result of **convection**, in which case the clouds make patterns of flat cumulus clouds that look like fish scales. This pattern is sometimes described as mackerel sky.

At other times the clouds are the result of bands of air moving upward. When this happens, cumulus clouds form in bands, with clear sky in between. The bands of clear sky distinguish cumulus from **stratus cloud**. Altocumulus clouds are often a sign of fair **weather**.

▶ **Altocumulus**—Compare the altocumulus in the foreground with the cumulonimbus cloud in the distance.

▼ **Altocumulus**—Altocumulus is produced when unstable air is shallow. Cumulus clouds begin to form but cannot grow due to warm air above them.

Condensation level

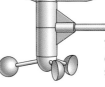

The blade at the top acts as a wind vane. The smallest end faces the wind.

◄ **Anemometer**

The three cups at the bottom catch the wind and spin the shaft around.

Altostratus

Layer clouds of medium height. The **clouds** are thin and often give a watery look to the sky because they only partly block out the Sun. They are sheets of cloud with no bands of clear sky in between. While not making **rain** themselves, altostratus clouds often signal the approach of a **weather front** and rain.

▼ **Altostratus**—Altostratus is often shown as a thin "watery" sky.

Anemometer

An instrument for measuring **wind** speed. It consists of three cups mounted on a central tube. As the wind fills the cups, they spin around, and the speed of rotation is used to measure the wind. In modern anemometers the speed is shown on a digital scale, and the data is usually entered directly into a computer for processing.

Anticyclone

Part of the lower **atmosphere** in which the air is sinking and flowing outward in a broad, gentle spiral. These **winds** move clockwise in the Northern Hemisphere and counterclockwise in the Southern Hemisphere. Because anticyclones are regions of **high-pressure** air, they are often called **highs**. Anticyclones often signal **settled weather**.

Because an anticyclone contains sinking air, thick **stratus clouds** or deep **cumulus clouds** do not occur. In summer the sky in an anticyclone may be clear, and this lets daytime **temperatures** rise. Ground heating may cause **convection**, but the sinking air prevents anything larger than tiny (fair weather) cumulus clouds from forming. If the air is moist, the weather can be dry yet overcast. In winter anticyclones allow air to lose **heat** to space. This can let **frost** and **fog** form. If the air cools enough, a thin blanket of cloud may also develop. This kind of cold, dull, windless, and monotonous weather is sometimes called "**anticyclonic gloom**."

In the **midlatitudes** some places have anticyclonic weather much of the time. Places where this happens lie around the **subtropics** and include the **Azores-Bermuda high**. **Poleward** of these semipermanent highs, anticyclones are formed by the way the air flows. These anticyclones (sometimes called **ridges** of high pressure) travel around the Earth with **depressions**, giving affected regions spells of settled weather between periods of depression **rain**.

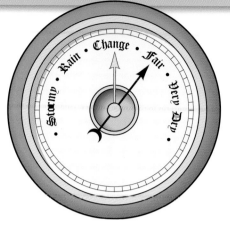

▲ **Anticyclone**—A barometer shows an anticyclone when the needle points to "Fair" or "Very Dry."

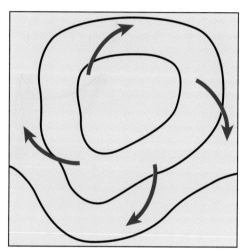

▼▶ **Anticyclone**—Anticyclones are regions marked HIGH on weather maps. They are areas of outward-spiraling and sinking air.

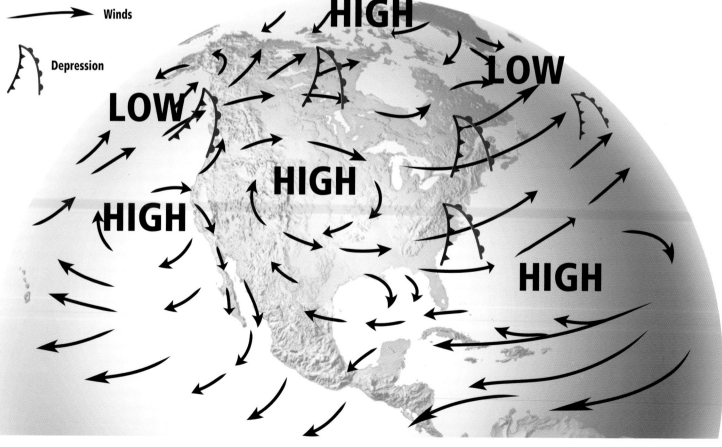

Winds

Depression

HIGH

LOW

LOW

HIGH

HIGH

HIGH

▼ **Anticyclone**—Summer anticyclones typically produce a sunny day with only cirrus clouds in the sky. Slightly poor visibility caused by dust in the air shows as haze toward the horizon.

◄▼ **Anticyclone**—A yellow or purple sunset is characteristic of anticyclonic conditions, especially in autumn and winter.

▼ **Anticyclone**—Seasonal high-pressure regions develop in extreme northerly continental locations in winter and produce prolonged periods of clear skies. This allows the ground to lose heat by radiation and so cool down greatly. The cold ground, in turn, cools the air in contact with it, reinforcing the tendency for the air to sink, and thereby prolongs and intensifies the anticyclone.

▲ **Anticyclone**—Radiation fog is typical of night and early morning conditions.

Anticyclonic gloom

Prolonged, dull, cold, windless conditions produced by **anticyclones** in winter. They are common over continental areas in the **midlatitudes**.

Arctic air

The **air stream** that flows down from the Arctic Ocean. It is a cold and often raw air stream, most common in winter and often connected with **rain**, **sleet**, and **snow** showers.

Arctic climate

A **cold climate** with a very brief warm **season** of fewer than three months above 6°C.

Arctic front

The region where an **arctic air** stream meets warmer air flowing **poleward** from the south.

Depressions are formed along this **front**.

Arctic sea smoke

Advection, or **steam fog**, in arctic waters. It occurs where air moving from the south flows over cold arctic waters.

Arid climate

Often called **desert climates**— where dryness is the overriding feature, and where plants are very scarce. There is no special amount of **rainfall** that marks these climates. They are determined entirely by the amount of vegetation that can grow.

Aspect

The direction something faces. In **weather** terms it is most important for mountain valleys in relation to the Sun. Places with an aspect facing the morning Sun become **frost**-free earlier in the day. Places with an aspect facing the setting Sun have warmer evenings.

Atmosphere

A shell of gases that surrounds the Earth. It is divided into many zones, each of which is important to people. The lowest zone, called the troposphere, contains all the **clouds**; the zone above, called the **stratosphere**, contains **ozone** gas that helps shield us from harmful **radiation** from the Sun.

Cold air sinks over the pole and moves back to the equator.

These winds carry cold air back to the equator.

These winds carry warm air toward the poles.

Rising moist air over tropical oceans causes thunderstorms nearly every day.

In this region the air sinks throughout the year, and little rain falls. This is where most deserts are found.

Warm air from the Tropics meets cold air from the poles in this region of the midlatitudes. Here the weather is very changeable, with periods of cloud and rain mixed with settled weather.

This region is so cold that little snow falls. However, because the snow that does fall rarely melts, snow and ice build up to cover the surface.

Atmospheric pressure

The weight of the air above a given point. It is also called barometric pressure and is measured in millimeters of mercury using a **barometer**. A place where the **air pressure** is greater than normal can be called a **high-pressure** region or **anticyclone**; a place where the pressure is lower than average can be called a **low-pressure** region, a **depression**, or **cyclone**.

Aurora

Also known as "northern lights" and "southern lights." It appears as shining folded curtains in the winter sky at high latitudes.

▲ **Aurora**—The colors of the aurora are produced when the charged particles of the solar wind are captured by the Earth's magnetic field. They collide with oxygen and nitrogen atoms in the upper atmosphere, emitting light, of which green, white, red, and blue are the most common.

◄ **Atmosphere**—This diagram shows the way in which the winds move across the Earth. Hot air rises over the equator, and cold air sinks over the poles. Hot and cold air mix in the midlatitudes to make changeable weather.

Azores-Bermuda high

The **subtropical high** usually positioned over the North Atlantic Ocean, level with North Africa. Stronger in summer than in winter, it shifts its position between the region of the island of Bermuda, in the west, and the islands of the Azores in the east. This **high** influences the track of **depressions** across the Atlantic Ocean. (*See also:* **Anticyclone**.)

B

Barometer

An instrument that measures the **pressure** of the **atmosphere** and is used in **weather** forecasting. There are two kinds of barometer. The most accurate kind uses a column of mercury. It is known as a Fortin barometer. The most common kind uses a thin-walled metal can from which the air has partly been sucked out. It is called an aneroid barometer.

Barometric pressure

(*See:* **Atmospheric pressure**.)

▼ **Barometer**—The aneroid barometer works by amplifying changes in the size of a partially evacuated bellows using a set of levers.

▲ **Atmosphere**—A satellite picture of Earth from space shows Africa with clouds over the equator (center) and clear skies over the deserts (top).

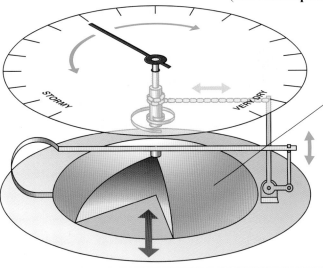

Sealed capsule is compressed during high pressure and expands as the pressure drops.

STORMY

VERY DRY

Beaufort scale

A scale for measuring **wind** speed in units from force 0 (**calm**) to force 12 (**hurricane** force).

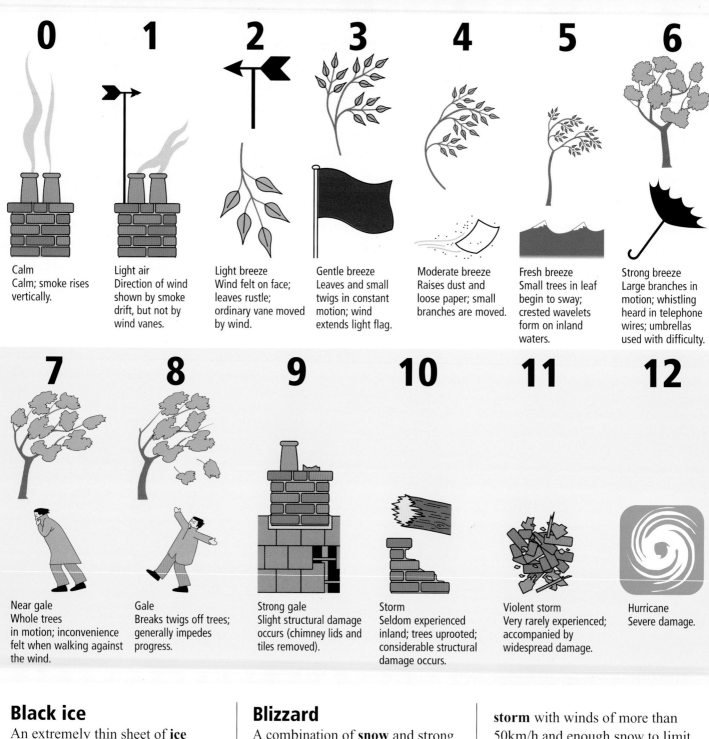

0
Calm
Calm; smoke rises vertically.

1
Light air
Direction of wind shown by smoke drift, but not by wind vanes.

2
Light breeze
Wind felt on face; leaves rustle; ordinary vane moved by wind.

3
Gentle breeze
Leaves and small twigs in constant motion; wind extends light flag.

4
Moderate breeze
Raises dust and loose paper; small branches are moved.

5
Fresh breeze
Small trees in leaf begin to sway; crested wavelets form on inland waters.

6
Strong breeze
Large branches in motion; whistling heard in telephone wires; umbrellas used with difficulty.

7
Near gale
Whole trees in motion; inconvenience felt when walking against the wind.

8
Gale
Breaks twigs off trees; generally impedes progress.

9
Strong gale
Slight structural damage occurs (chimney lids and tiles removed).

10
Storm
Seldom experienced inland; trees uprooted; considerable structural damage occurs.

11
Violent storm
Very rarely experienced; accompanied by widespread damage.

12
Hurricane
Severe damage.

Black ice

An extremely thin sheet of **ice** that develops on winter roads but cannot be easily seen since the black road surface (tarmac) continues to look normal. It occurs when air **temperatures** fall below about 3°C and is a driving hazard. (*See also:* **Glaze**.)

Blizzard

A combination of **snow** and strong **wind** such that the snow moves almost horizontally and causes severe snow drifts. Definitions of blizzards vary between countries. The term blizzard was first used in the central United States, where such conditions are common in winter. The United States Weather Service defines a blizzard as a **storm** with winds of more than 50km/h and enough snow to limit **visibility** to 150m or less. A severe blizzard occurs when winds exceed 72km/h, visibility is near zero, and **temperatures** fall below -12°C. In other countries, such as the United Kingdom, where blizzards are much less common, the term is used for any combination of heavy snow and strong winds.

Blustery

A description of a **wind** that changes speed unpredictably, but which is always moderate or strong.

Bora

A cold **wind** that blows from the north or northeast plains across the lands around the Adriatic Sea. It is most common in spring.

Breeze

A low-speed **wind** that can be classified as light, gentle, moderate, fresh, or strong (**Beaufort scale** 2 to 6).

Buster

A sudden, violent, and cold **wind** that blows from the south across Australia (alternatively referred to in parts of Australia as a "southerly buster" or a "brickfielder"). It occurs on the eastern side of the Great Dividing Range.

C

Calm

No apparent movement of the air (**Beaufort scale** 0).

Calms

A region close to the equator where there is no reliable prevailing **wind**, and where the air often moves very sluggishly. This, combined with the high **humidity** and **temperature** of the air, makes the region of calms very oppressive. (*See also:* **Doldrums**.)

Ceiling

A word used to describe the height of the base of the **clouds** on a cloudy day. The height is given in meters.

Chinook

A **foehn** type of downslope **wind** in which moist wind from the Pacific Ocean first moves over the Rocky Mountains, where it loses much of its **moisture**, then sinks over the frozen plains of the northwestern United States and Canada, warming and drying further as it does so.

It often melts several centimeters of **snow** within a few hours. That is why the chinook is also called the "snow-eater."

Circulation

The way in which air moves within the **atmosphere**. In general, air moves from regions of **high pressure** to regions of **low pressure** and from places where it is hot to places where it is cold. The spin of the Earth causes the flow of air to take on curved or spiraling patterns, especially in the **midlatitudes**.

Cirrocumulus cloud

High-level, thin, white **clouds** made of **ice crystals**, often forming into regular ripples or bands across the sky. They are often the first clouds to be seen in advance of the arrival of a **weather front**.

Cirrostratus cloud

Thin layers of high, white **clouds** made of **ice crystals**. When seen through this very thin cloud, the Sun may appear to have a halo. In fact, the halo may be the only thing to indicate the presence of the cloud if it is extremely thin. Most cirrostratus clouds signal cold winter conditions and are often moving ahead of a **weather front**.

Cirrus cloud

Cirrus **clouds** are thin, veil-like, or wispy **ice** clouds that form high in the **atmosphere**. They are composed of **ice crystals**. They are normally a sign of fair **weather**.

◄ **Cirrus cloud**—Cirrus cloud has a typically wispy character. It is always seen against an otherwise clear blue sky.

City weather

The warmer conditions that exist within a city due to the shelter of buildings and the heat produced by heating systems and vehicle exhausts. (*See also*: **Heat Island**.)

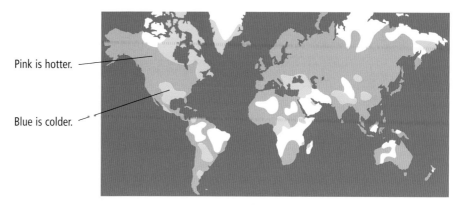

Pink is hotter.

Blue is colder.

Climate

The long-term, or average, kind of **weather** that might be expected at a particular place over time. To find out the climate of a place, long-term readings are taken of **temperature**, **rainfall**, **cloud** formation, and so on, and averages are figured out for each month. (*For types of climate see individual entries.*)

Climatic change

The world's **climate** has changed both slowly and quickly during the three billion years since the **atmosphere** formed. However, at the moment the atmosphere appears to be warming very quickly. This may be due to natural processes, or it may be due to human activity such as burning

▲ **Climatic change**—This map shows which places seem to be getting hotter and which seem to be getting colder due to global warming.

fossil fuels. When people use the term "climate change" today, they mostly mean change due to people, although there is no conclusive proof as yet that people are responsible for the change.

▼ **Climate**—The Earth's main climate types.

Hot climates:
- Equatorial and Tropical marine
- Tropical continental and Monsoon

Dry climates:
- Hot dry with seasonal rain
- Cool dry with dry winter
- Desert

Warm subtropical or temperate climates:
- Dry winter
- Rain throughout year
- Dry summer

Cool temperate climates:
- Marine
- Continental

Cold climates:
- Continental

Polar and mountain climates:
- Arctic
- Ice
- Mountain

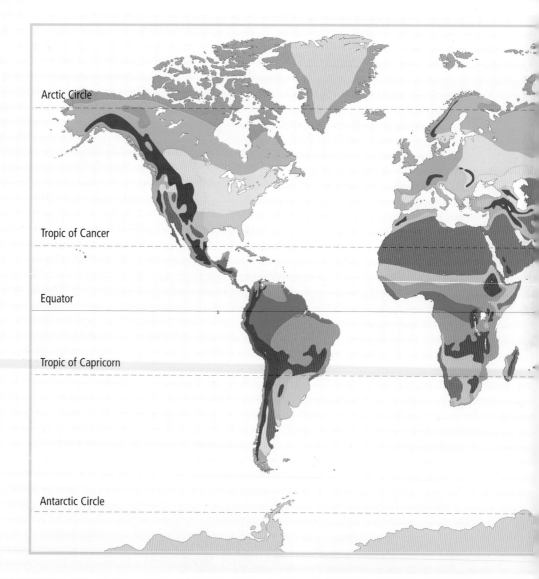

Arctic Circle

Tropic of Cancer

Equator

Tropic of Capricorn

Antarctic Circle

Cloud

A large number of water droplets or **ice crystals** suspended in the **atmosphere**. The water or ice partly blocks out the Sun, so that the cloud appears as a white to dark gray mass in the sky.

(*For types of cloud see:* **Alto-**; **Altocumulus**; **Altostratus**; **Cirrocumulus**; **Cirrostratus**; **Cirrus**; **Cumulonimbus**; **Cumulus**; **Layer cloud**; **Nimbostratus**; **Nimbus**; **Stratocumulus**; **Stratus**.)

Cloudburst

Used to describe very sudden, heavy **rainfall** such as would come from a summer **thunderstorm**.

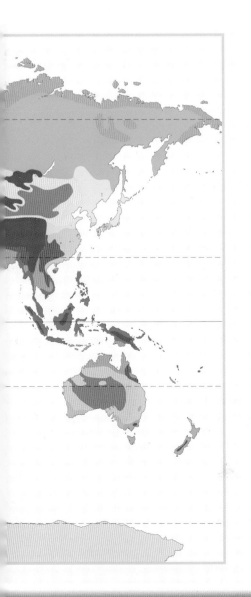

Col

A region of the **atmosphere** between two **high-pressure** or two **low-pressure** areas. There is little **wind**, and the **weather** is often dull and slow to change.

Cold climate

Where there is a long cold **season** lasting between six and nine months.

Cold front

The boundary between warm and cold air near the rear of a **depression**. Ahead of the **front**, in the warm part of the depression, the air is warmer than anywhere else in the depression. The air generally sinks, or at least does not rise, so shallow **cloud** is all that forms.

At a cold front cold air undercuts warm air in a depression. The undercutting lifts the warm air and makes all the air cool. This may cause some of the air to shed its **moisture** as droplets of water. As it does this, **heat** is released, and the lower part of the cloud may warm enough to rise of its

own accord, forming large amounts of tall **cumulus cloud** called **cumulonimbus**. Heavy, **squally rain** then follows. Behind the cold front lies cold air that has come from the poles. This air warms in its lower layers as it moves, and pockets of warmed air rise, causing cumulus clouds to form and showers to follow.

The **weather** behind a cold front is typically **sunshine** and showers with a cold or fresh **wind**.

(*See also:* **Depression**.)

Condensation

The process in which **moisture** or vapor changes to liquid water when it comes into contact with cold surfaces, or when air is lifted to cold, high parts of the **atmosphere**. A common form of condensation on the ground is **dew**. In the air condensation takes place on floating microscopic particles of dust. They grow into water droplets, which are seen as **cloud**. Condensation releases some heat, which keeps the air from cooling very rapidly. (*See also:* **Fog**.)

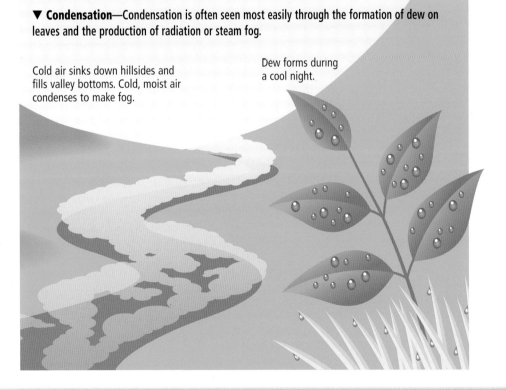

▼ **Condensation**—Condensation is often seen most easily through the formation of dew on leaves and the production of radiation or steam fog.

Cold air sinks down hillsides and fills valley bottoms. Cold, moist air condenses to make fog.

Dew forms during a cool night.

Conduction

The transfer of **heat** between two substances that are touching.

For example, as cold air flows over a warm sea, the air brushing against the sea begins to warm up. (This warmed air may then be transferred to higher levels by **convection**.)

Continental climate

A **climate** experienced in places far from the ocean, or where **winds** blow constantly offshore. Typical effects of a continental climate include maximum amount of **rainfall** in the summer and large variation between summer and winter **temperatures**.

Convection

The process whereby air turns over due to being heated from below.

Warm air is less dense than cold air and so will rise through cold air. If air is warmed near the ground, it will begin to rise through the **atmosphere**, usually in the form of **thermals**. This may cause the formation of **cumulus clouds**. To balance the rising air, cold air sinks between the thermals. This cold air is cloud-free, explaining why cumulus clouds are separated by patches of clear sky.

Convectional rain

Rain, often torrential, from **thunderstorms** (**convectional** thunderstorms) that have been produced by moist air rising vertically from the surrounding heated land or ocean surface (convectional activity).

Cool temperate climate

A **climate** in which the **seasons** (spring, summer, autumn, and winter) change mainly due to **temperature**, and in which there is

▲ **Cumulonimbus cloud**—Cumulonimbus clouds are the typical storm clouds of summer, as here over the Great Plains.

a cold season (below 6°C) of one to five months.

Cool temperate climates can be **maritime** (western margin, with maximum **rainfall** in the winter) or **continental** (eastern margin, with maximum rainfall in the summer).

(*See also:* **Cold climate** and **Warm climate**.)

Cool temperate, dry climate

Dry climates that have hot summers and cold winters. They have unreliable summer **rainfall** that often results in scrubby vegetation. Steppe, prairie, pampas, and veld are all names for vegetation zones in the **midlatitudes** connected to dry climates.

Cumulonimbus cloud

A very deep form of **cumulus cloud**, mainly linked to **thunderstorms**. **Nimbus** means rain-bearing (*see:* **Virga**). The biggest cumulonimbus clouds form over very hot continents, where there is a flow of moist air. The Great Plains region of the United States has many cumulonimbus clouds in summer, when warm, moist air is sucked from the Gulf of Mexico and heated daily by the strong summer **sunshine**. Cumulonimbus clouds often signal **tropical cyclones** and the **cold front** of a **depression**. All tropical rainclouds are of the cumulonimbus kind.

The level at which the moisture in the parcel of rising air condenses to form the cloud.

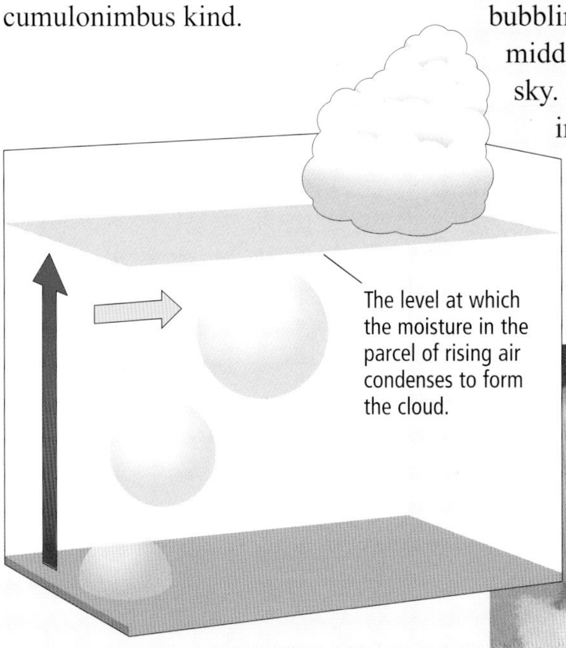

▲ **Cumulus cloud**—The diagram shows how air rises to form cumulus clouds.

Warm bubbles of air rising from the warm ground gradually get colder. Although they are still warmer than the surrounding atmosphere, the cooling bubbles cannot hold all of the moisture they had when nearer the ground, and at a certain height some of it condenses onto tiny particles of dust floating in the air.

Air bubbles remain invisible until the critical height is reached, and then condensation occurs. This height is the bottom of the cloud.

If the cloud becomes thick, the water droplets and ice crystals will grow big enough to fall from the air as rain or snow.

Cumulus cloud

Individual **clouds** that form in a sky when warmed air is rising.

They are especially dramatic in the **tropics** and in the centers of **midlatitude** continents during the hot summer **season**, when they can bring downpours and spawn **tornadoes**. Cumulus clouds are formed by **convection currents** and tend to form on a daily basis when there is strong **sunshine** and moist air. The day may start fine and clear, but ground heating soon occurs, and this **heat** is transferred by **conduction** to the lower layers of air. This warmed air then begins to rise, so that cumulus clouds are bubbling up by midmorning. By midday the clouds may cover the sky. Cumulus clouds fade away in the late afternoon because the Sun is lower in the sky and can no longer heat the ground strongly.

Current

A concentrated flow of air, such as a **jet stream**, or a concentrated flow of water, such as the **Gulf Stream**.

Cyclone

A large area of the **atmosphere** where the air is swirling inward and upward in a corkscrewlike manner. Air spirals counterclockwise in the Northern Hemisphere and clockwise in the Southern Hemisphere. **Depressions** are actually weak cyclones, but that term is usually used only for **tropical cyclones** (called **hurricanes** in the Americas and **typhoons** in the West Pacific).

The causes of depressions and tropical cyclones are completely different, however.

▼ **Cumulus cloud**—Heated land often acts as the trigger for moist air flowing in from the sea. This is a typical summer situation in Miami.

D

Depression

A **midlatitude cyclone** or "**low**" carried by the **westerly winds**. Warm tropical air and cool **polar air** are drawn together. Where the cold and warm air meet, zones of activity, called **fronts**, occur. The leading front is called a **warm front**, and the trailing zone of activity is called a **cold front**.

The cold, denser air cuts under the warm, less dense air. As the warm air rises, it cools, producing broad bands of **cloud** and **rain** (or **snow**) along the frontal zones. Within a **depression** air spirals counterclockwise in the Northern Hemisphere and clockwise in the Southern Hemisphere.

Depressions are constantly forming, maturing, and decaying as they travel westward around the world. Each depression is steered by a fast-flowing region of air called the **jet stream**, which is located high in the **atmosphere**. By tracking the jet stream, **weather** forecasters are able to predict the movement of the depressions and their accompanying clouds and rain.

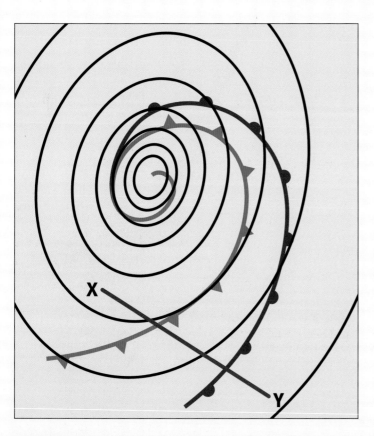

▲▼ **Depression**—In a depression isobars are more closely packed than in an anticyclone, and winds blow inward and counterclockwise.

The diagram below shows a cross section through X to Y shown above. The main cloud bands are associated with the two fronts. The warm front (of which the main cloud is nimbostratus) is normally the wider front, but the cold front (where the main cloud is cumulonimbus) is steeper and often contains the more severe weather. In the warm sector a thin layer of stratus cloud often obscures the sky.

▲ **Depression**—Here you see the symbols for warm and cold front drawn over a satellite picture that shows the spiraling pattern of cloud in a depression.

| X | Cold front | Warm sector | Warm front | Y |

Cold front

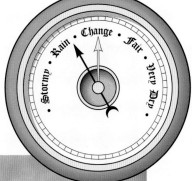

▲ **Depression—**
Cold front cloud.

Warm sector

▶ **Depression—**
Warm sector cloud.

Warm front

▶ **Depression—**
Warm front cloud.

Desert

Regions with very low **rainfall** and extremely sparse vegetation.

Deserts cover about a sixth of the Earth's land surface. They fall into three groups: **hot desert climates**, cold **desert climates**, and **rain-shadow** deserts.

Desert climate

Very **dry climates** where the amount of **precipitation** is so low that very little vegetation can grow. **Hot desert climates** are those with no average monthly **temperature** below 6°C. Cold desert climates are those with at least one cold month (average temperatures below 6°C).

▼ **Desert climate**—Dunes are found in areas where wind-blown sand builds up.

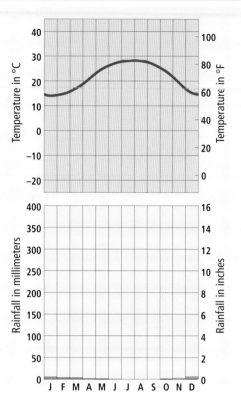

▶ **Desert climate**—Cairo in Egypt has no month with significant rain.

Dew

Moisture that settles on grass and other surfaces when air cools. The **temperature** at which dew forms is called the **dew point**. (*See also:* **Condensation**.)

Dew point (dew-point temperature)

The **temperature** at which air becomes saturated with **moisture** and starts to form water droplets.

Diurnal

Daily, as something that occurs in or lasts one day.

Doctor, the

A regular, cool onshore **wind** that blows over a warm coastal area in southwestern Australia. In southern South Africa this type of wind is called the Cape Doctor.

Dog days

A term used in North America for a period of very hot, sultry summer **weather** that often occurs when the Dog Star, Sirius, is visible in the night sky.

Doldrums

A zone of **calms** in the equatorial regions of the world's oceans that moves slightly north or south with the **overhead Sun**. It usually features daily **thunderstorm rain**.

Downdraft

A **wind** caused by rapid downward movement of air in a thundercloud (*see:* **Thunderstorm**).

Drizzle

Light **rain**. Drizzle is a feature of weak **depressions**, especially **warm fronts**.

Drought

The term for an unusually long period without significant **rainfall**.

Some parts of the world, particularly between latitudes 1° and 20°, have a more variable

▼ **Drought**—During a drought water levels may fall so far that rivers dry up, and water has to be sought from below the river bed.

rainfall pattern than others, and so they can be said to be more drought-prone.

These places include the **Sahel** region of Africa just south of the Sahara Desert, southern Africa, northeast Brazil, Australia, southern California, the southwestern U.S., and India. The **Dust Bowl** in North America is a drought-prone area of about 400,000 sq km.

Dry climate

Where the principal feature is that **evaporation** and **transpiration** greatly exceed **precipitation** at all times of the year. (*See also*: **Cool temperate climate**; **Desert climate**; **Hot dry climate**.)

▲ **Dust storm**—The start of a dust storm in Morocco.

Dust Bowl

Part of the Great Plains of North America, centered on Oklahoma, which suffered such a terrible **drought** in the 1930s that much of the topsoil blew away, and many farmers had to abandon their land.

Dust devil

A localized spiraling of air on a hot day.

Dust storm

A strong **wind** that picks up dust (soil) from fields to such an extent that it reduces **visibility** dramatically. (*See also*: **Haboob**.)

E

El Niño

The name given to a global change in the world's **weather** that occurs about every four years. At this time **storms** and **droughts** are much more frequent, especially in areas within or close to the **tropics**.

◄ **El Niño**—This red area shows the places where the Pacific Ocean changes. It is a long band off the coast of Peru. A huge amount of water is involved, covering an area of surface water the size of Europe.

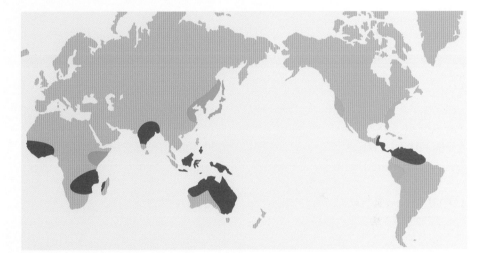

▲ **El Niño**—This map shows the places in the world most affected by El Niño. Notice how eastern Australia and southeast Asia suffer drought (red), as do India and southeast Africa, while northeast Africa, Peru, and California experience torrential rainstorms (green).

◄ **El Niño**—Disastrous fires are an important El Niño effect. In recent years widespread fires have raged in El Niño drought areas, for example, Australia and Indonesia.

Equatorial climate

A **hot climate**, with **rain** in every month, and with two periods of maximum rain just after the time when the **overhead Sun** crosses the equator. **Temperatures** vary by fewer than 5°C throughout the year. (*For features of equatorial climates see:* **Doldrums**; **Equatorial low**; and **Supercells**.)

Equatorial low

A zone of **low-pressure** air that encircles the Earth in the **tropics**, and whose position is influenced by the **overhead Sun**.

Equinox

The two times of the year when the midday Sun is **overhead** at the equator, and the length of day and night are the same everywhere in the world. This happens in March and September.

Evaporation

The loss of water from the surface due to the drying effect of the air.

Evapotranspiration

The loss of water from plants, bodies of water, and ground surfaces due to the twin processes of **evaporation** (on water and ground) and **transpiration** (on plants). It is a more accurate description of the amount of water lost from forests and fields than evaporation.

Eye

The central, **calm** region of a **tropical cyclone**. The eye may be just 2 to 3km across, compared with the diameter of the **storm**, which may be over 500km. There is no **cloud** over the eye, while all around the cyclone contains raging **winds** and torrential **rain**.

Eye wall

The towering **clouds** that make the edge of the **eye** in a **tropical cyclone**.

F

Fill, filling

When a **cyclone** is weakening, and **air pressure** is rising, **weather** forecasters say that the **depression** is filling.

Foehn

A dry, warm **wind** that blows down the **leeward** side of mountains. It is caused as winds flow across mountains, warming as they descend. The name foehn is given to the warm winds that blow over the European Alps, where the ferocious winds create a roaring sound. The **chinook** is the name for a similar wind that blows down the eastern slopes of the North American Rocky Mountains.

Fog

Cloud that forms at ground level. Cold sea or land conditions make the air cool, and some of the **moisture** in it condenses into tiny water droplets (*see:* **Condensation**). The more water droplets that form, the thicker the fog. The thinnest form of fog is called **mist**. (*See also:* **Advection fog** and **Radiation fog**.)

▶ **Fog**—Fog is the result of a combination of low temperatures and moist air. Valley bottoms are places where cold air builds up during the night, while moisture from a warm river may feed extra vapor into the air. As a result fogs form first and last longest over rivers.

Freezing point

The **temperature** at which water turns to **ice**. It is usually 0°C.

Freezing rain

When **rain** falls onto frozen surfaces, it often freezes, creating sheets of **ice**. This often happens in winter in **midlatitudes** when a **depression** blows over an area that has been below freezing for many days.

Friagem

A cold, antarctic **wind** that blows across southerly regions of South America in the **lee** of the Andes. It moves with the trailing edge of a passing **depression** (similar to a North American **norther** or an Australian **buster**).

Front

Used in **meteorology** to describe the boundary between two types of air in the **atmosphere**. Fronts are nearly always marked by a broad

belt of **cloud** and **rain**. Fronts can be **warm fronts**, **cold fronts**, or **occluded fronts**. An observer can recognize a warm front because the air changes from cold to warm, while a cold front produces a change from warm to cold air.

An **occluded front** is usually marked by cold air becoming quickly colder. Warm fronts are

broader and make less intense rain than cold fronts.

(*See also:* **Depression**.)

Frost

Occurs when **moisture** in the air freezes onto surfaces, producing a thin film of **ice crystals**.

Freezing normally occurs when the **temperature** of the surface falls to 0°C. (*See also:* **Hoar frost** and **Rime**.)

G

Gale

A strong **wind** blowing between force 7 (near gale) through force 9 (severe gale) up to force 10 (full gale or **storm**) on the **Beaufort scale**.

▶ **Greenhouse effect**—The Sun's rays can reach the ground without being absorbed by the air. However, radiation from the ground is reflected by clouds and absorbed by carbon dioxide and water vapor in the air, so less gets out than comes in, and the air heats up.

▲ **Frost**—As moisture-laden air blows gently past the cold surfaces, it forms ice crystals.

Glaze

A coating of **ice** due to **freezing rain** or to rain that freezes overnight, when **temperatures** are often lower. (*See also:* **Black ice**.)

Greenhouse effect

The gradual warming of the world's **atmosphere** due to the increase in the amount of carbon dioxide in the air.

Gulf Stream

A warm ocean **current** that begins in the Gulf of Mexico and then moves across the surface of the North Atlantic Ocean and nears the Atlantic coast of North America before turning east and spreading out to cross the Atlantic Ocean. As soon as it begins to cross the Atlantic Ocean, it is called the **North Atlantic Drift**.

Gust

A short blast of air.

H

Haboob

Very strong **desert winds**, usually accompanied by **dust storms** in the Sudan in Africa and in the Sonoran Desert of southern Arizona.

Hail, hailstones

A pellet of **ice** that is formed inside a tall **cumulus cloud**. A hailstone starts as a **raindrop** that has frozen when carried high enough by **wind** in the **cloud**. The falling hailstone collects **moisture** that forms a new layer of ice as the stone is again lifted through the cloud. Many layers of ice may be added until the hailstone is heavy enough to fall to the ground. Some hailstones have grown to weigh over half a kilo.

Harmattan

A very hot **wind** that blows southwest from central Africa and can bring clouds of stinging dust.

Haze

A condition of the air in which **visibility** is reduced by the buildup of dust particles in it. It usually happens during dry conditions, because **rainfall** washes particles from the air. An extreme form of haze over cities involves particles of **pollution** and is called **smog**.

Heat

The part of the Sun's energy that causes the **temperature** to rise.

▼ **Hailstones**—Hailstones are often pea-sized as here, but may be larger than the size of oranges.

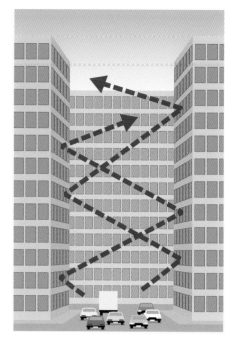

▲ **Heat island**—Tall buildings trap heat, reflecting it back and forth and preventing the air from losing as much heat as in other parts of the city.

Heat island

The region in and around a city that remains up to several degrees warmer than the surrounding countryside on still summer nights and during **calm** spells in winter. The extra heat comes from buildings, industry, and traffic. The amount of warmth varies with the size of the city and with the speed of the **wind**. The extra heat tends to disappear when winds rise above 20km/h.

▼ **Heat island**—The thermometers show how the center of a city is warmer than the countryside around it.

Heat wave

A few days of unusually hot **weather**. **Heat** waves are a feature of the **midlatitudes** and result from a tongue of tropical air moving **poleward**. Heat waves happen only in the summer.

High

A region in which the **air pressure**, as measured by a **barometer**, is higher than average. Highs are places of sinking air and clear, **settled weather**. Also used as a shorthand for **high-pressure** system, or **anticyclone**.

High pressure

The buildup of air in some parts of the **atmosphere**. It is often used as an alternative to **anticyclone**.

Hoar frost

Frost that occurs when there is both **wind** and very moist air. Hoar frost can build up to be many centimeters long.

Horse latitudes

The part of the Atlantic Ocean where the winds change from westerly to easterly. They exist near 30°N and 30°S, and make up a zone of plentiful **sunshine** and long **calms**. (*See also:* **Doldrums**).

▲ Hot climate—Places with a hot climate and long dry periods are often favored tourist destinations.

Hot climate

Where it is always hot, and average monthly **temperatures** do not fall below 18°C. There are **equatorial climate** and **tropical climate** types, including **tropical continental climate**, **tropical marine climate**, and **tropical monsoon climate**.

◀ Hoar frost—Hoar frost has built up on thin cattle wire to make this fence look as though it is solid.

Hot desert climate

Where it is hot and permanently under the influence of **trade winds** blowing over the land. (*See also:* **Desert climate**.)

Hot dry climate

Dry climates of the **tropics** and **subtropics**, which may have a short period of unreliable seasonal rain, often part of a summer **monsoon**. These regions are characterized by a sparse vegetation of grass and small trees, called scrub. (*See also:* **Hot climate**.)

Humidity

The amount of **moisture** in the air. The full term is relative humidity, which means the amount of moisture in the air compared with the maximum amount that the air could hold. If the relative humidity is close to the maximum that the air can hold, little moisture evaporates from the skin, and the air feels sticky and uncomfortable (humid). High **temperature** combined with high relative humidity can pose a serious threat to health. High humidity, wind, and low temperatures make the air feel very "raw."

When air holds as much water vapor as possible, the relative humidity is said to be 100%.

Hurricane

A very fierce, damaging **wind** of the **tropics** and **subtropics**. The general term hurricane also refers to a **tropical cyclone** in North America (**Beaufort scale** 12+). (*See also:* **Eye**; **Eyewall**; and **Hurricane-force winds**.)

▼ **Hurricane**—As the winds spiral in a hurricane, they form regions of upward-moving air separated by regions where air moves downward. Where the air is moving up, huge walls of cumulonimbus clouds form. In the center of the hurricane is the clear region called the eye.

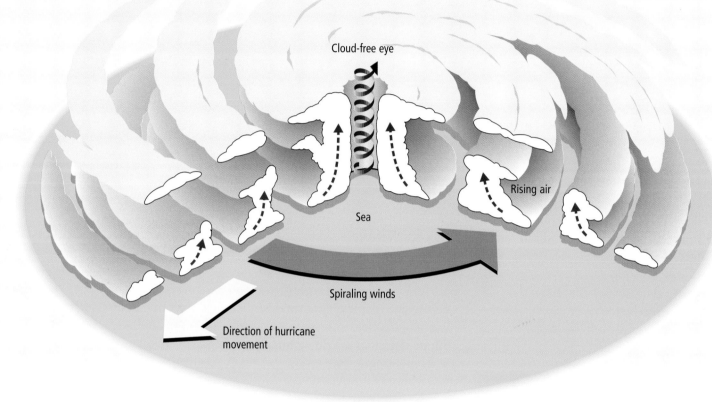

Cloud-free eye

Rising air

Sea

Spiraling winds

Direction of hurricane movement

Hurricane-force winds

Winds whose speeds exceed 117km/h.

I

Ice

The solid form of water. Sheets of ice often develop on land where **rain** occurs on cold ground.

Ice climate

A very cold, **polar climate** with average monthly **temperatures** never climbing above 6°C. Characterized by permanent **ice** and permafrost, a layer of frozen ground that never thaws.

◄ **Ice**—Surface ice is a common phenomenon in winter for places that have long cold spells separated by warm, rainy weather. The rain freezes on the frozen ground, making driving hazardous.

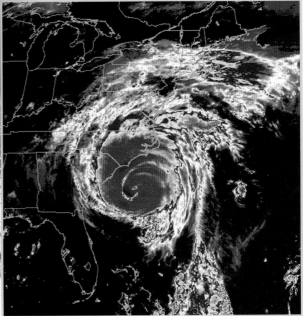

▲ **Hurricane**—The central eye region and spiraling clouds show well from space. Notice how the central region (where the air is rising most strongly) has some of the tallest clouds.

Ice crystals

Also known as **snowflakes**, they are small particles of **ice** that usually form in **clouds** when **temperatures** in the cloud drop too low for water to remain liquid. The temperature at which ice crystals form depends on the **air pressure**. High up in a cloud temperatures are well below 0°C.

Icelandic low

The part of the **atmosphere** between Iceland and Greenland, in the North Atlantic Ocean, where **low-pressure** systems, or **depressions**, are formed, or where they grow stronger. It is strongest in winter.

Indian summer

Used in the **midlatitudes** to describe an autumn interlude of good, warm, summerlike **weather**. The expression is borrowed from the **climate** of the Indian subcontinent, where sunny, warm weather in September and October follows a period of heavy **rain**.

Inversion

The opposite of the normal way in which air gets cooler with height. In an inversion the coolest air is near the ground, and the warmer air is higher up.

Isobar

A line drawn on a **weather** chart (*see:* **Synoptic chart**) to represent places having the same **atmospheric pressure**.

You can think of isobars as invisible shapes in the air. The closer together the isobars are, the steeper the slope of **pressure** in the air, and the faster the air will flow from **high pressure** to **low pressure**. The faster the air flows across isobars, the stronger the **wind** will be. As a result, isobars can help predict where regions of strong winds will occur.

▼ **Isobar**—Isobars are lines of equal pressure on synoptic charts marking areas of highs and lows.

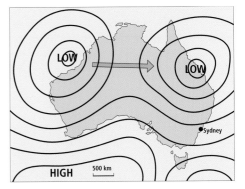

Isohyet

A line drawn on a **weather** chart (*see:* **Synoptic chart**) to represent places having the same amount of **rainfall**.

Isotherm

A line on a **weather** chart (*see:* **Synoptic chart**) that joins places with the same **temperature**.

J

Jet stream

A tunnel of fast-moving air that normally forms where two different kinds of air meet high in the **atmosphere**. There are two jet streams in each hemisphere, one near the Arctic or Antarctic Circle (called the **polar jet stream**), the other close to the **tropics** (called the subtropical jet stream).

K

Khamsin

A hot, dry **wind** that blows from the Sahara **Desert** to Egypt. It is known as *rih al khamsin* ("the wind of 50 days") in North Africa and the Arabian Peninsular, an indication of how long it lasts. (*Khamsin* is the Arabic word for 50.)

L

Land breeze

A **breeze** that blows off the land toward the sea. Land breezes are common when nice, sunny, **settled weather** occurs during the night, when the land has cooled down more than the nearby sea. Air rises over the sea, drawing cooler air off the land. It is the opposite of a **sea breeze**.

Latitude

The distance north and south of the equator measured in degrees and often shown on maps as a line. The equator is at 0°, the North Pole is 90°N, and the South Pole is 90°S.

Latitudes are also used to mean the bands of similar **weather** that occur at certain distances between the equator and the poles (for example, **midlatitudes**).

Layer cloud

Clouds that are formed by the bulk upward movement of moist air. This happens when air moves up over cold air at a **front** and also on the **windward** side of a mountain. Layer clouds are always of the **stratus** type.

◄ **Lightning—** Lightning strikes between the base of the cloud and the ground. This is a time-exposure photograph; only one or two strokes would occur at any one instant.

Lee, leeward

The coast or flank of a mountain sheltered from the prevailing **winds**. The lee side of a mountain is useful as a sheltered harbor, but it may present problems for farming, since lee sides lie in the **rain shadow** of mountains and so may be quite dry.

Local weather

The special **weather** effects that show up when the air is **calm**. Examples include **mountain and valley winds**, **sea breezes**, and **heat islands**.

Low, low pressure

A region in which the **air pressure**, as measured by a **barometer**, is lower than average. Lows are places of rising air, **cloud**, and **rain**, and cause **depressions** or **cyclones**.

▼ **Lightning**—Lightning is the world's greatest display of the discharge of static electricity.

Lightning

A natural spark between layers in a **cloud** or between a cloud and the ground.

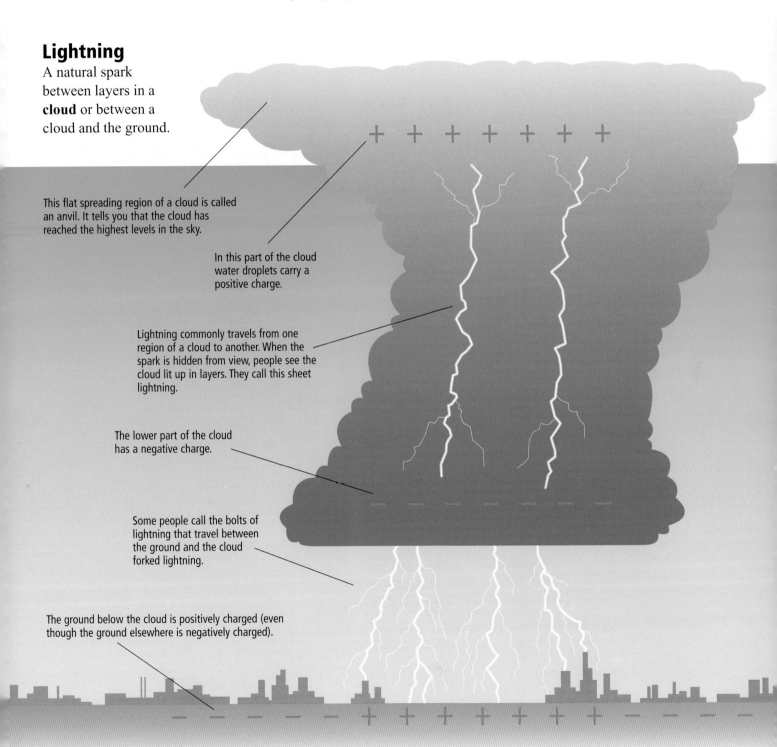

This flat spreading region of a cloud is called an anvil. It tells you that the cloud has reached the highest levels in the sky.

In this part of the cloud water droplets carry a positive charge.

Lightning commonly travels from one region of a cloud to another. When the spark is hidden from view, people see the cloud lit up in layers. They call this sheet lightning.

The lower part of the cloud has a negative charge.

Some people call the bolts of lightning that travel between the ground and the cloud forked lightning.

The ground below the cloud is positively charged (even though the ground elsewhere is negatively charged).

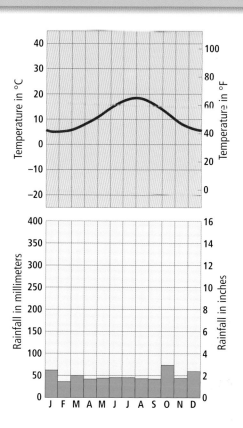

◄ **Maritime climate**—A maritime climate, whether hot or cold, is characterized by an evenness of rainfall and temperature.

M

Maritime climate

A **climate** that is influenced by being close to a large body of water, usually an ocean, and that experiences onshore **winds**. The **heat**-absorbing properties of the ocean cause the range of temperatures through the year to be much smaller than in the center of continents.

Maritime climates are noted for being mild and humid (*see:* **Humidity**). Examples are the Pacific coast of North America, northwestern Europe, southern Chile, southeastern Australia, and New Zealand.

Mediterranean climate

A **warm temperate** coastal **climate** with a hot, dry summer and a mild, wet winter. The term comes from the Mediterranean region of Europe, but similar climates are found in southern California, central Chile, South Africa, and southern Australia.

▲ **Mediterranean climate**—Mediterranean climates have about six months with virtually no rain or cloud. Humidity is also low, and despite the high daytime temperatures, the weather feels comfortable. This combination is attractive to vacationers.

Meteorology

The study of the Earth's **atmosphere** and, in particular, the patterns of **weather**.

Midlatitudes

Those parts of the Earth that lie between the Tropic of Cancer (23.5°N) and the Arctic Circle, and between the Tropic of Capricorn (23.5°S) and the Antarctic Circle. (*For weather features of the midlatitudes see:* **Anticyclone**; **Anticyclonic gloom**; **Circulation**; **Cumulus cloud**; **Freezing rain**; **Heat wave**; **Indian summer**; **Prevailing westerly winds**; **Stratus cloud**; and **Westerlies/ westerly winds**.)

Millibar (mb)

A unit of **air pressure** used in the metric system. A bar (1,000mb) represents the average pressure of the air at sea level. It is equal to 760mm of mercury.

Places where the pressure is significantly higher than this are said to have **high pressure**, while places with a pressure significantly lower than this are said to experience **low pressure**. The lowest known pressure was 870mb, measured in the **eye** of a **typhoon** near Guam in October 1979. Intense **depressions** normally have centers no lower than 960mb.

Mirage

An optical effect seen over hot, dry land, where it appears that there is a shimmering body of water. This illusion is caused by hot air rising over the land.

Mist

A mass of tiny water droplets suspended in the air that makes it difficult to see long distances. (Compare with **haze**, which is due to dust.) When the **visibility** is reduced below 1km, **fog** occurs. Both mist and fog happen because the **temperature** of the air has been cooled enough to force some of the **moisture** to condense (*see:* **Condensation**) into water droplets, forming **cloud** at ground level.

Mistral

A dry and cold **wind** that blows from the cold Swiss plateau through the Rhone Valley of France during spring. It can cause great crop damage if it occurs in late spring.

Moisture

Water vapor. Water vapor is a gas. When the vapor is cooled, it condenses (*see:* **Condensation**) to form liquid water, **dew**, or **cloud**.

Monsoon

Any seasonal **wind** that blows toward a continent in summer and away from it in winter. Used only in connection with places that have distinct wet and dry **seasons**.

Countries that experience monsoons are all within, or close to, the **tropics**. The monsoon is particularly characteristic of India, where its arrival can usually be predicted within a few days, ending a period of intense **heat**, and bringing welcome cooler air and heavy rains. About half of the world's population depends on the rains brought during the monsoon for the successful growth of their crops.

▶ **Monsoon—**Towering clouds herald the outbreak of the monsoon over Bombay, India.

▶ **Monsoon—**The characteristic rainfall chart for a monsoon climate shows a sudden start to the rainy season. Temperatures dip slightly at the same time because of the high cloud amounts.

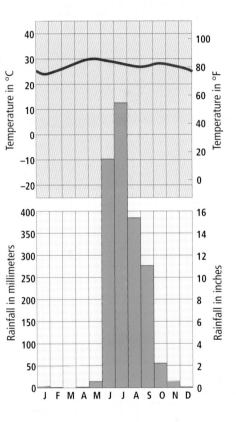

◀ **Monsoon—**People do their best to adapt to the monsoon, but flooding and suffering are inevitable.

▲ **Monsoon—**The Indian monsoon is often likened to a giant sea breeze, with hot, moist winds being sucked from the ocean over a very hot continent.

Mountain and valley winds

Local **winds** experienced in mountain areas on a daily basis during clear **weather**. They are due to the different amounts of **heat** received, or lost, by the mountains and valleys.

Mountain winds blow down to the valleys at night; valley winds blow up toward the mountains during the day.

▲ **Nimbostratus**—Nimbostratus is the rain cloud that accompanies the passage of a warm front, so that the sky is full of cloud.

Mountain climate

The special **climate** experienced in mountains due to their height. Most mountains have a wetter climate on the side facing the prevailing wind and a dry, sometimes **desert climate** on the **lee**, or **rain-shadow**, side.

Mountains are also notorious for their extremely variable **weather**. This usually applies to places above 1,300m.

(*For other features of mountain weather see:* **Adret**; **Aspect**; **Foehn**; **Friagem**; **Mountain and valley winds**; **Orographic effect**; and **Windward**.)

N

Nimbostratus

Thick **layer clouds** capable of producing **rain**. Nimbostratus clouds are formed at **fronts**, where a large bank of air is lifted up, forcing the uplifted air to cool. The cooled air cannot hold all of its water as vapor, so the water vapor forms droplets at low levels and **ice crystals** at very high levels. As the gentle air **currents** waft water droplets into the upper levels of the **cloud** that contain ice, the **raindrops** freeze onto the ice crystals, making them larger. These large crystals are then big enough to fall from the cloud. As they fall, they melt and turn into raindrops. Nimbostratus clouds do not have any **thunder** or **lightning**. Once thunder and lightning start, the clouds are called **cumulonimbus**.

◄ **Mountain climate**—The rapid variability of mountain weather is seen here. The pictures were taken just five minutes apart.

▶ **Orographic effect**—This picture of Hawaii shows the way that clouds build up over the mountains while leaving the coast bathed in sunshine.

Nimbus

Meaning **rain**-bearing, and referring to **clouds**: **cumulonimbus** is used for tall thunderclouds; **nimbostratus** for thick, rain-bearing **layer clouds**.

North Atlantic Drift

A warm ocean **current** that flows across the North Atlantic Ocean from the east coast of North America (where it is called the **Gulf Stream**) and warms the coasts of northwest Europe.

Northeaster, noreaster

A strong (often **gale**-force) **wind** that blows across New England from the northeast.

Norther

A cold winter **wind** that sweeps south from the Canadian prairies across the southern United States and then out over the Gulf of Mexico. It is often pulled south behind passing **depressions**. A norther may reach a speed of 60km/h, and it often makes the air very dusty.

O

Occluded front, occlusion

A kind of **weather front** that exists in some **depressions**. An occlusion occurs when the cold air in a depression completely lifts the warm air off the ground. The result is the formation of one wide belt of **rain**-bearing **cloud**, instead of the two bands that normally separate **cold fronts** and **warm fronts**.

Orographic effect, relief effect

This is the effect that mountains have on **rainfall**. Air flowing toward a mountain range is forced to rise to cross the mountains. This lifting makes the air cool, and often **clouds** and rain are produced. This rain is in addition to the rain that might otherwise fall had there been no mountain range.

Overcast sky

A sky that is covered with gray **clouds**, usually **layer**, or **stratus**, clouds.

Overhead Sun

The position of the Sun at midday. Also means the place on Earth where the Sun is directly overhead at midday and therefore where the Sun's heating is greatest. The global **weather** between the equator and the poles is closely related to the position of the overhead Sun through the year and is the reason why they vary in a predictable way with the **seasons**.

Ozone

A form of oxygen molecule consisting of three atoms of oxygen formed in the upper **atmosphere**. It absorbs incoming ultraviolet rays from the Sun. In places where ozone is thin, exposing the skin for long periods in sunny **weather** can be a health hazard.

P

Pacific high

The **subtropical high** that dominates the Pacific Ocean. Particularly strong in the North Pacific, off the west coast of North America. Stronger in summer than in winter.

Pampero

A cold southerly **wind**, similar to the **norther**, but occurring east of the Andes in Argentina.

Photochemical smog

(*See:* **Smog**.)

Polar air

A cold, dry **air mass** that forms over the centers of northerly continents in winter and also over Antarctica.

Polar climate

Very **cold climates** of the high latitudes, where the average temperatures in the warmest month do not rise above 10°C.

Polar front

The line that separates cold **polar air** from tropical air in the **midlatitudes**. **Depressions** form along this **front** and then move eastward.

Polar jet stream

A tunnel of very fast-moving air that encircles the Earth high in the **atmosphere**, close to the **poleward** limit of the **midlatitudes**. It forms into great waves as it moves. These waves influence where **depressions** and **anticyclones** will appear in the midlatitudes. In general, anticyclones emerge on parts of the waves that turn toward the equator, while the parts of the wave that turn toward the pole are the sites of strings of depressions.

Poleward

Moving in the direction of (or toward) the North or South Pole.

Pollution

Any addition of a significant amount of material into the air that disrupts the natural environment. Atmospheric pollution is mainly in the form of acidic gases such as sulfur dioxide (which cause **acid rain**), dust particles (which cause **haze**), and carbon dioxide (which causes the **greenhouse effect**).

(*See also*: **Smog**.)

▶ **Pollution**—Los Angeles is among many places that suffer from photochemical smog in summer.

Precipitation

Liquid and solid water that falls or condenses (*see*: **Condensation**) from the air—**rain**, **snow**, **hail**, **dew**, and so on.

Pressure

The weight of the **atmosphere** on a given area. The terms **high pressure** and **low pressure** refer to the **air pressure** in the part of the atmosphere near the ground. A region of high pressure is formed where air **currents** cause air to sink over a region of the Earth, thus adding to the weight of the air. A region of low pressure is an area where air is rising, counteracting the normal weight of the air.

Pressure systems

The **lows** (low-pressure systems) and **highs** (high-pressure systems) in the **atmosphere**.

Prevailing westerly winds

Winds that blow across the **midlatitudes** from west to east. They contain **depressions** and **anticyclones**, and signal changeable **weather**. Also called **westerlies/westerly winds**.

R

Radiation

The transfer of **heat** through space and the **atmosphere** by the vibration of atoms. The **weather** is entirely driven by the heat energy that is radiated from the Sun. Heat is lost from the atmosphere and from the surface of the Earth by radiation. This is especially noticeable at night, when heat is lost by radiation if the sky is cloudless.

Clouds can reflect (bounce back) radiation. That is why heat is kept in on a cloudy night, and why a cloudy day is colder than a sunny day.

Radiation fog

A type of **fog** caused by the ground cooling, usually overnight. Radiation fog is seen over rivers and in the bottoms of valleys, where the cold air gathers over moist surfaces.

Radiosonde

A set of instruments that are carried aloft by a helium balloon so that the conditions of the **atmosphere** can be measured. The measurements are transmitted electronically, using a small radio.

The information is sent back to a ground receiving station.

The most common observations made by radiosonde are **temperature**, **humidity**, and **pressure**.

Radiosondes are an important aid to **weather** forecasting.

Rain, raindrop, rainfall

Small droplets of water that surround a fine particle of dust, crystal of salt, or some other solid object. Raindrops fall through the air when they are heavy enough to fall against the rising air that is inside a **cloud**. When the air is rising slowly, as in the clouds at the **warm front** of a **depression**, the raindrops only need to be of modest size (1mm diameter or less) to fall out to the ground. Such fine rain is called **drizzle**. As the rising air gets more powerful, the droplets have to be larger before they can fall. In a thundercloud (*see:* **Thunderstorm**) the rising air **currents** are strong, so that drops

Particle

▶ **Rain**—Raindrops begin as small droplets of water that condense on particles of dust or, in the case of cold clouds, on ice crystals.

▼ **Rainfall**—Rain is falling from the center of this isolated cumulonimbus cloud. The streaks of rain, called virga, are clearly seen, although the rain never reaches the ground because the air below is so dry that the droplets evaporate as they fall.

have to be very large to fall out—often several millimeters across. That is why raindrops from large **cumulus** thunderclouds are bigger than those from **layer clouds**.

Many raindrops begin life as **ice crystals**. That is because clouds are very cold, and ice forms in their highest levels. As ice crystals lock together, they form large shapes called **snowflakes**. As the snowflakes fall, they begin to melt

and eventually turn into raindrops. This is probably the most common way for raindrops to form in layer clouds. In cumulus clouds raindrops are swept together in the powerful air currents until they become big enough to fall from the sky.

As raindrops fall from the sky, they change shape. They begin as spheres; but as they fall, air resistance makes them flatten and then become "doughnut shaped." No raindrops are ever teardrop shaped, as mistakenly shown in some diagrams.

Rainbow

A rainbow is a colored arc that stretches across the sky when **sunshine** hits **rain** falling from a nearby **cloud**. The colors in the rainbow split all of the colors present in white light into separate bands. This is called a spectrum.

The rainbow is produced by the way the light is caught by the millions of **raindrops** in the cloud. Sunlight enters each tiny raindrop and is bounced around inside (a process scientists call refraction). While this is happening, the various colors in the white light become separated, so that when the light finally emerges from the

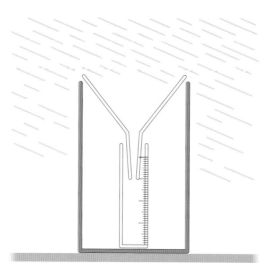

▲ **Rain gauge**—A rain gauge is a funnel that leads down to a measuring cylinder.

raindrop, it is split up into a spectrum of colors.

It is possible to see a number of rainbows at the same time, the lowest one being the brightest, and higher ones getting progressively fainter. This is also caused by the way light is changed as it enters raindrops.

Rain gauge

An instrument for measuring **rainfall**. The design of a rain gauge is important, and each country has its own variation on a standardized shape of rain gauge. All designs have some common

◄▼ **Rainbow**—The complete visible spectrum of colors shows in a rainbow. The inset picture shows a principal rainbow, with further, fainter rainbows outside it. They occur because the raindrops internally refect some light several times before allowing it to escape.

features: A funnel is placed so that its rim is level. The funnel gathers water and sends it to a collecting bottle. From time to time (often once a day) the total rainfall in the bottle is measured.

Automated rain gauges can send electronic signals giving the amount of rainfall and provide information on rainfall in real time.

Rain shadow

A region with relatively low **rainfall** because it is sheltered from the prevailing **winds** by mountains or hills. As the winds rise up the **windward** side of the high land, they cool and release most of their **moisture**. The now drier winds also warm up as they descend on the **lee** side, and this combination makes rainfall more scarce. **Deserts** often lie in the permanent rain-shadow regions of the world's highest mountains. Much of Tibet, which lies in the rain shadow of the Himalayas, is desert.

Relative humidity

(*See:* **Humidity**.)

Relief effect

(*See:* **Orographic effect**.)

Relief rain

The result of moist air being forced to rise as it passes over high land (a relief). All **winds** are capable of producing relief rain as they move from ocean to land, but the amount of rain depends on the height of the relief, and some low-lying areas may get no rain from these winds.

Ridge

A term used in connection with **high pressure**. A ridge of high pressure is a region of high pressure that separates two **depressions**. It signals a short period of good **weather** between two unsettled spells.

Rime

A form of **frost** in which a thick coating of **ice crystals** builds up on leaves, twigs, and fences. (*See also:* **Hoar frost**.)

S

Sahel

A **semiarid** region of North Africa between the Sahara **Desert** and the savannas to the south. Characterized by a short and unreliable wet **season** and a long dry season. Very prone to **drought**.

Santa Ana

A hot, dry **wind** that flows from the Great Basin, between the Sierras and the Rocky Mountains, and into the Los Angeles Basin of California, **gusting** to over 100km/h. It often fans brush fires.

Saturated air

Air that holds as much **moisture** as possible. The relative **humidity** of saturated air is 100%.

▼ **Relief rain**—The windward side of a mountain range experiences far more precipitation than the lee side.

The windward side of a mountain is the slope facing the wind. As the air rises and cools, it releases moisture as droplets and forms cloud.

Snow

Snowline

Rain

The sheltered, or lee, side of a mountain receives less rain than the windward side. This is called the rainshadow.

Sea breeze

A coastal **wind** caused by the heating effect of the land relative to the sea. During a hot day the land heats up, and the air in contact with it becomes less dense and rises. This, in turn, sucks in cold air from the sea. At night the land may become cooler than the sea, in which case an offshore wind (**land breeze**) develops.

▼ **Sea breeze**—Sea breezes forming clouds just inland of the coast.

▼ **Sea breeze**—This diagram shows the way that a sea breeze is produced. Notice that the breeze is set up because the land is warmed, causing the warmed air to rise. Cool air flows in from the sea to take the place of the rising warm air. This is an example of convection.

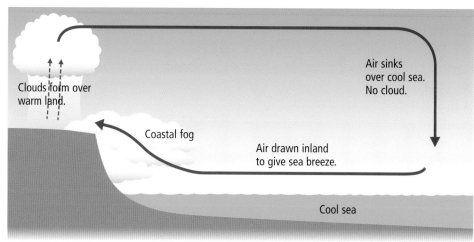

Clouds form over warm land.

Air sinks over cool sea. No cloud.

Coastal fog

Air drawn inland to give sea breeze.

Cool sea

Season

A period of the year that has a marked character (for example, summer is hot; a dry season has very little rain).

▼ **Season**—The tropics experience seasons because of the movement of the overhead Sun. Because the Sun is always high in the sky, all places are hot; seasons are created by rain.

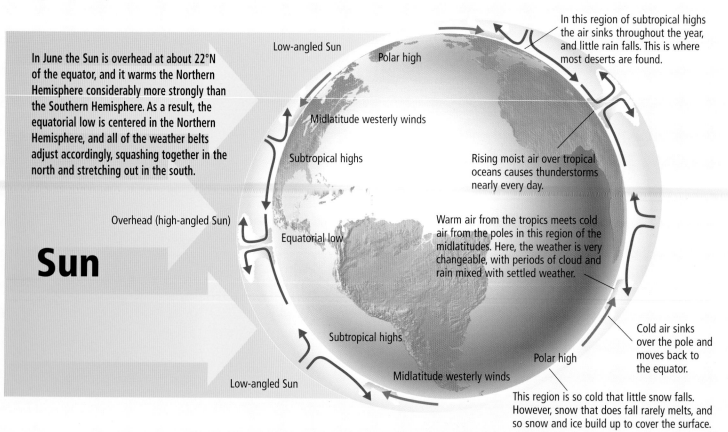

In June the Sun is overhead at about 22°N of the equator, and it warms the Northern Hemisphere considerably more strongly than the Southern Hemisphere. As a result, the equatorial low is centered in the Northern Hemisphere, and all of the weather belts adjust accordingly, squashing together in the north and stretching out in the south.

Low-angled Sun

Polar high

Midlatitude westerly winds

Subtropical highs

Overhead (high-angled Sun)

Equatorial low

Sun

Low-angled Sun

Subtropical highs

Midlatitude westerly winds

In this region of subtropical highs the air sinks throughout the year, and little rain falls. This is where most deserts are found.

Rising moist air over tropical oceans causes thunderstorms nearly every day.

Warm air from the tropics meets cold air from the poles in this region of the midlatitudes. Here, the weather is very changeable, with periods of cloud and rain mixed with settled weather.

Cold air sinks over the pole and moves back to the equator.

Polar high

This region is so cold that little snow falls. However, snow that does fall rarely melts, and so snow and ice build up to cover the surface.

Semiarid climate

A **climate** of low **rainfall** characterized by irregular and unpredictable rainy **seasons**.

Semiarid regions often form on the edges of **deserts** or in **rain-shadow** basins. They are more risky than deserts because, from time to time, there is enough rainfall to support farming, which provides hope and encouragement to farmers. As a result, they may overdevelop their land. Then, when the **weather** changes to a period of less rain (often described as "when the rains fail"), catastrophe may follow.

The **Sahel** of Africa is a region of semiarid climate with a large population where disasters due to rain failures are common. The Great Plains region of North America is also a semiarid region. The disaster that produced the **Dust Bowl** was due to a period of low rainfall and overdevelopment.

Settled weather

When the sky is clear, and **sunshine** (in warm **weather**) or **fog** (in cold weather) is most likely. (*See also:* **Anticyclone**.)

Siberian high

The **high** positioned over north and central Asia in winter.

Simoom

The Arabian equivalent of the **Harmattan wind**. Simoom means "poison wind."

Sirocco

A dry, hot **wind** from the Sahara, which can blow dust and sand across the Mediterranean. It is equivalent to the **khamsin**. It is pulled north into the warm sector of **depressions** moving over the Mediterranean Sea during autumn and spring. Air **temperatures** may exceed 40°C and approach 50°C.

Sleet

A form of **freezing rain**. Sleet is made of small pellets of **ice** that form when **raindrops** fall through a layer of air whose **temperature** is below freezing.

Smog

A **fog** or **haze** intensified by atmospheric **pollution**. Smog affected by sunlight is called photochemical smog. The term was first applied to the fogs that plagued industrial cities such as Pittsburgh and London in the coal-burning era of the 19th and early 20th centuries. It is now used for the photochemical smogs that develop over cities such as Los Angeles and Mexico City. These cities have sunny **weather** and lie in basins that block most **winds**. The main polluters are motor vehicles.

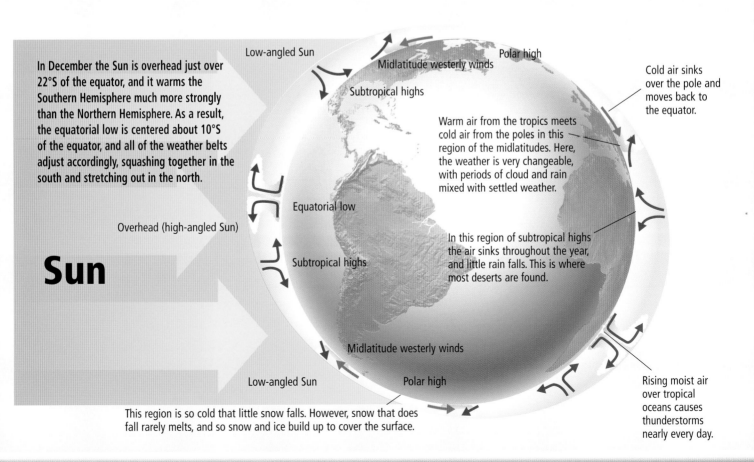

In December the Sun is overhead just over 22°S of the equator, and it warms the Southern Hemisphere much more strongly than the Northern Hemisphere. As a result, the equatorial low is centered about 10°S of the equator, and all of the weather belts adjust accordingly, squashing together in the south and stretching out in the north.

Overhead (high-angled Sun)

Sun

Low-angled Sun

Midlatitude westerly winds

Polar high

Subtropical highs

Warm air from the tropics meets cold air from the poles in this region of the midlatitudes. Here, the weather is very changeable, with periods of cloud and rain mixed with settled weather.

Cold air sinks over the pole and moves back to the equator.

Equatorial low

In this region of subtropical highs the air sinks throughout the year, and little rain falls. This is where most deserts are found.

Subtropical highs

Midlatitude westerly winds

Low-angled Sun

Polar high

This region is so cold that little snow falls. However, snow that does fall rarely melts, and so snow and ice build up to cover the surface.

Rising moist air over tropical oceans causes thunderstorms nearly every day.

Snow

Small crystals of frozen water (**ice crystals**) high up in cold **clouds**. The crystals form a variety of six-pointed shapes. Also, the accumulation of ice crystals on the ground.

▶ **Snow**—Snow can be a major inconvenience where it drifts or lasts for many months.

▶ **Snow**—Snow cannot settle on steep slopes. Most of it is blown away and fills in valley bottoms.

Snowbirds

This term was first coined for people from the northern United States or Canada who spent the winter in the south each year to escape the snow and cold **weather** of the north. Also now applies to the seasonal migration of retired Australians and Europeans.

Snowflake

A group of **ice crystals** that have clumped together so they are sufficiently heavy to fall out of a **cloud**. Snowflakes may be several centimeters across.

▶ **Snowflake**—
Snowflakes show the characteristic six-pointed features of crystalline ice.

Squall

A sudden **storm** with **wind** speeds of 40km/h or more and lasting for at least two minutes, typically accompanied by **rain**, **snow**, or **sleet**. A squall line is a patch of stormy conditions that may accompany a **front**.

Steam fog

A kind of **advection fog** that forms when cold air moves over a warm, wet surface such as a warm ocean **current**. The air warms at the base by **conduction** and becomes saturated by the **evaporation** of **moisture** from the river, lake, or ocean. Because the bottom of the air becomes warm, it tends to rise by **convection**, and this carries the fog upward as it forms. This gives the appearance of rising steam or smoke. A common steam fog is **arctic sea smoke**.

Storm

Severe **weather** with heavy **rain** and strong **winds**. The most severe storms are **tropical cyclones**, also called **hurricanes** and **typhoons**. (*See also:* **Lightning**; **Thunder**; **Thunderstorm**.)

Storm-force wind

A very strong **wind** (**Beaufort scale** 10 and 11).

Stratocumulus cloud

Low-level white or gray **clouds** with a rolling, or rippled, appearance. They are not generally **rain** clouds because they are too thin. Higher-level clouds of the same kind are called **altocumulus**.

▲ **Stratocumulus cloud**—Stratocumulus cloud is seen as flattened cumulus, often in rolls.

Stratosphere

The part of the **atmosphere** above the region where **clouds** form. The stratosphere acts as a lid, keeping all the air turbulence and clouds close to the ground, in the layer called the troposphere.

▼ **Stratosphere**—In this picture the plane is flying in the stratosphere with the troposphere and its clouds and dust below.

Stratus cloud

Layer clouds, usually characteristic of **clouds** in the **midlatitudes** and high latitudes. Stratus clouds are dull gray. The thicker the cloud, the darker its color.

Typically, stratus clouds will form along the **fronts** of **depressions** and bring bands of prolonged **rain**. Stratus cloud at ground level is experienced as **fog**.

Stratus clouds have many names depending on their shape, their height, and the likelihood they will bring rains. When the word stratus cloud is used on its own, it refers to low-level cloud. Higher-level layer clouds have prefixes such as **alto-** (**altostratus**). There are also **stratocumulus**, **cirrostratus**, **cumulostratus**, and **nimbostratus**.

▼ **Stratus cloud**—Stratus cloud is the heavy, gray, featureless cloud that accompanies a weather front.

Subtropical climate

(*See:* **Warm temperate climate**.)

Subtropical high

A semipermanent region of **high-pressure** air that forms just **poleward** of the **tropics** at the **horse latitudes**. Such **highs** form mainly over the oceans and are

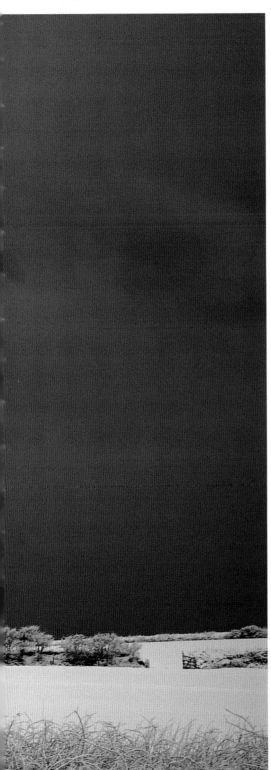

some of the most durable features of the yearly **circulation**. Most of these highs have names (e.g., **Azores-Bermuda high** in the North Atlantic).

Subtropics

The region on the **poleward** side of the **tropics**. The subtropics are also sometimes known as warm temperate regions.

(*For weather features of the subtropics see:* **Anticyclone**; **Azores-Bermuda high**; **Hot dry climate**; **Pacific high**; **Subtropical high**; **Trade winds**; **Warm temperate climate**.)

Sunshine

For **weather** purposes it is the **heat** energy from the Sun.

Supercells

Regions, usually over the warm oceans near the equator, in which clusters of **thunderstorms** form and eventually produce **tropical cyclones**.

Synoptic chart

Often known commonly as a "**weather** chart," it is the map that weather forecasters use to help predict and explain the weather. It shows the pattern of

isobars and also **weather fronts**. It is used for short-term predictions a few days ahead.

T

Temperate climate

A **climate** in which the main seasonal changes are due to **temperature**, but there is no long, cold winter.

Temperate also means a lack of extremes, so temperate climates are usually found in coastal locations under the influence of moderating onshore winds.

There are **cool temperate climates** and **warm temperate climates**.

Temperature

The amount of heat present, measured using a **thermometer**, and shown by a scale using °C (degrees Celsius). **Weather** reports normally give the temperature of the air measured in the shade.

Thermal

An upward-moving flow of warm air caused by ground heating. Most **cumulus clouds** form as a result of thermals.

▶ **Synoptic chart—** A synoptic chart shows the pattern of highs and lows. It is used for short-term weather forecasting. It is the type seen on news channels.

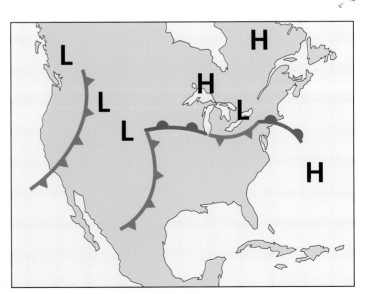

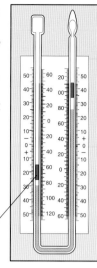

▶ **Thermometer**—This maximum-minimum thermometer records the highest and lowest temperatures of the day. The tube contains two small metal markers that are pushed up by the mercury as it moves around the U-shaped tube. The magnets are held in their farthest positions by a magnet behind the scale.

Metal marker

Thermometer

An instrument for measuring **temperature**. A number of different kinds of thermometer are used for recording the temperature of air in **weather** observations. Most commonly, a pair of thermometers is used to read the maximum and minimum temperatures that occurred during a day.

Because temperature is affected by the speed of air and the **moisture** in the air, different pairs of thermometers are used to measure the temperature in dry air and in wet air. They are called dry bulb and wet bulb thermometers (*see:* **Wet bulb temperature**). The wet bulb thermometer is wrapped with a small piece of muslin cloth, one end of which is dipped in water. As water evaporates from the muslin, it pulls heat from the bulb of the thermometer, and the apparent temperature falls. The wet and dry bulbs only read the same temperature when the air is saturated with water, for example, when it is raining.

Thunder

A loud, often rumbling sound that accompanies some severe **storms** in which **lightning** occurs.

A flash of lightning heats the air to about 30,000°C. This makes the air expand violently, sending shock waves outward that become a sound wave. It takes about three to four seconds for the sound of thunder to travel one kilometer, so it is possible to estimate the distance of the lightning flash by finding the time between seeing the flash and hearing the thunder.

The reverberating nature of thunder is caused by the sound waves echoing off the layers of the thundercloud (*see:* **Thunderstorm**).

Thunderstorm

A **storm** that is localized to a single thundercloud, which is linked with tall **cumulonimbus clouds**. The constant, rapid movement of air up and down inside such clouds is responsible for the formation of **lightning**, **thunder**, and large **raindrops** or **hail**.

Tornado

An extremely violent, tightly spiraling column of air that reaches down from the bottom of a giant thundercloud. Originally the Spanish word for **thunderstorm**, tornadoes are violently spinning funnels of air that follow the base of severe thunderstorm **clouds**. Tornado **winds** can reach over 400km/h or more. A tornado over water sucks water from the ocean and is called a **waterspout**.

▼ **Tornado**—A tornado darkens the skyline. Notice the scale given by the utility poles on the right.

▶ **Thunderstorm**—A thunderstorm is usually marked by very dark skies because thunderstorms result from great thicknesses of cloud that effectively block out sunlight.

▼ **Tornado**—In a tornado winds spiral upward and inward to create velocities of several hundred kilometers an hour, making it possible for a tornado to destroy buildings and lift the remains into the air. They are restricted to places with rapidly forming thunderstorms such as "Tornado Alley" that runs across the southern United States.

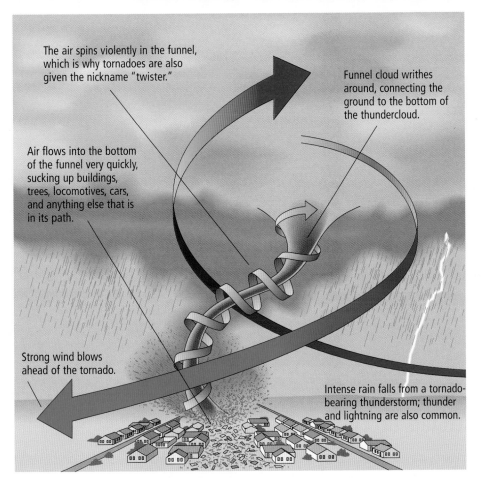

The air spins violently in the funnel, which is why tornadoes are also given the nickname "twister."

Air flows into the bottom of the funnel very quickly, sucking up buildings, trees, locomotives, cars, and anything else that is in its path.

Funnel cloud writhes around, connecting the ground to the bottom of the thundercloud.

Strong wind blows ahead of the tornado.

Intense rain falls from a tornado-bearing thunderstorm; thunder and lightning are also common.

Tornado watch

A government observation network designed to give warning of **tornadoes**.

Trade winds

Winds that blow constantly from the **subtropical highs** toward the equator. The trades are caused by wind flowing out of the **high-pressure** zone at latitude 30° toward the **low-pressure** zone at the equator. In the Northern Hemisphere the trade winds blow from the northeast (northeast trade winds). In the Southern Hemisphere they blow from the southeast (southeast trade winds). They tend to bring **rain** when they blow onto an easterly coast and **drought** when they blow off a westerly coast.

The trade winds are the most reliable winds in the world. In the days of sailing ships they could be guaranteed to carry ships on their routes carrying goods between countries, hence the name trade winds.

▶ **Trade winds**— The trade winds are so named because of their reliability for trade in times when people relied on sails.

Transpiration

The release of water vapor into the air by plants as they respire (take in carbon dioxide and give out oxygen).

Tropical climate

Climates mainly between 30°N and 30°S of the equator are considered tropical. They include the tropical rainforest (equatorial) climate, the **monsoon** climate, the savanna climate, and the main areas of **desert**.

Tropical continental climate

A **hot climate** in which the average monthly temperature never falls below 18°C. Dry **seasons** occur at the time when the **trade winds** blow, and wet **seasons** of thundery **weather** correspond with the influence of the **equatorial low**.

Tropical cyclone

A deep **low-pressure** region that originates in the **tropics**, and that develops spiraling **hurricane-force winds**. Tropical cyclones are called **hurricanes** in the Americas and **typhoons** in the North Pacific. (*See also:* **Eye** and **Eye wall**.)

Tropical marine climate

A **hot climate** in which the **trade winds** bring **rain** for part of the year, and the **equatorial low** dominates for the rest of the year, bringing **calm weather** but daily **thunderstorms**. Mainly affects tropical islands.

Tropical monsoon climate

A **hot climate** in which the average monthly temperature does not fall below 18°C, and the wet **season** corresponds to a time when moist air flows onshore from the neighboring hot ocean. **Monsoon** climates have higher **rainfall** than those that simply experience an ordinary wet season.

Tropics

The part of the Earth that lies between the Tropic of Cancer (23.5°N) and the Tropic of Capricorn (23.5°S).
(*For weather features of the tropics see:* **Albedo**; **Cumulus cloud**; **Cumulonimbus cloud**; **Cyclone**; **El Niño**; **Equatorial low**; **Hot dry climate**; **Jet stream**; **Monsoon**; **Tropical climate**; **Tropical cyclone**; **Tropical marine climate**.)

Tropopause

The boundary between the lower part of the **atmosphere** that contains all of the **clouds** and **weather** (the troposphere) and the higher part of the atmosphere (the **stratosphere**) that acts like a lid, keeping the weather below it.

Trough of low pressure

A part of the **atmosphere** where two **low-pressure** regions make a lozenge-shaped region of low pressure.

Twister

Another name for a **tornado**.

Typhoon

The name in the West Pacific for a **tropical cyclone** with winds of over 120km/h. A typhoon is an alternative name for **hurricane**.

V

Veer

A **wind** that shifts in a clockwise direction. Often noticeable as a **weather front** passes through.

Virga

Trails of **rain** seen falling from the base of the **cloud** but which evaporate (*see:* **Evaporation**) before reaching the ground.

Visibility

The distance that can be seen clearly. **Haze**, **smog**, **mist**, and **fog** may all reduce visibility.

▲ **Virga**—Virga are the long trails of rain seen coming from the bottom of a thundercloud.

W

Warm front

A sloping boundary between cold and warm air in a **depression**. It is a place where **cloud** and **rain** are most likely.

This is the sequence of events that an observer would see as a warm front approaches:

First, **cirrostratus clouds** are seen high in the sky. Over the next few hours the clouds become lower and thicker. Cirrostratus clouds block out the Sun only slightly, creating a halo effect around it. As lower, thicker clouds appear, the Sun is more hidden. **Altostratus clouds** produce a watery-looking sky, then finally, **stratus clouds** obscure the sky completely.

If a large amount of air is lifted up behind the **front**, the cloud formed in the air above the front will be very thick and dark gray. It will be **nimbostratus cloud**, and rain will fall from it.

(*See:* **Depression**.)

Warm temperate climate

Where there is **rain** at all times of the year, and where there are **seasons** based on **temperature**, but in which there is no cold season (no month with temperatures below 6°C). Also sometimes called a **subtropical climate**. Warm temperate climates on the eastern coasts of continents get their maximum rainfall in summer; those on the western coasts get their maximum rainfall in winter and are called **Mediterranean climates**. Warm temperate climates can also experience **monsoons**.

▶ **Water cycle—**
The water cycle is the continuous circulation of moisture between the land, oceans, and atmosphere.

Water cycle

The way in which **moisture** circulates as gas, liquid, or solid between the land and the air.

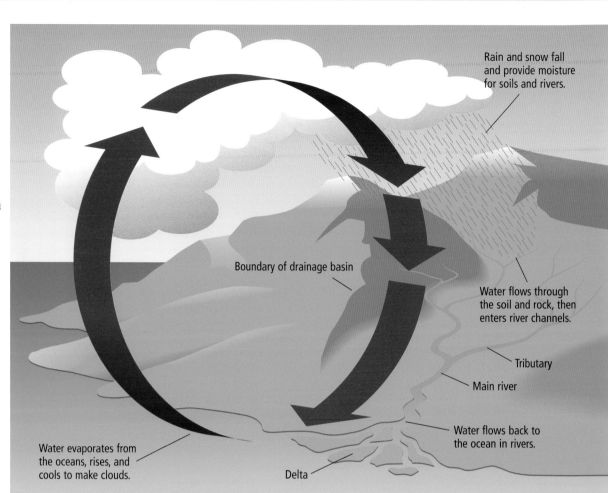

Rain and snow fall and provide moisture for soils and rivers.

Boundary of drainage basin

Water flows through the soil and rock, then enters river channels.

Tributary

Main river

Water flows back to the ocean in rivers.

Water evaporates from the oceans, rises, and cools to make clouds.

Delta

Waterspout

A **tornado** over water.

Weather

The nature of the **atmosphere** as we experience it each day.

This is best understood by the way that the word is used. People ask, "What will the weather be like tomorrow?" and mean what will the **temperature** be, how **cloudy** or sunny will it be, will it **rain**, or will it be **windy**? These are all properties of the atmosphere, measured by weather forecasters. Contrast this with the word **climate**, which is the long-term average of all the weather records over many years. For example, people go on vacation to places that have a sunny climate, knowing that the day-to-day weather is, on average, likely to be warm and sunny.

Weather chart

(*See:* **Synoptic chart**.)

Weather front

The sloping region where air of two different kinds meets. It is a place of **cloud** and **rain**. There are **cold fronts** and **warm fronts**. (*See also:* **Cirrocumulus cloud**; **Cirrostratus cloud**; **Depression**.)

Weather hazard

Conditions that put lives and property at risk. They include heavy **rain**, causing landslides and floods, **hurricanes**, **tornadoes**, and **droughts**.

Westerlies/westerly winds

This is the name for a broad zone in the **midlatitudes** where **winds** blow most frequently from the west. Also linked to the westerlies are the surface **depressions** that bring **storms** and the **jet stream**.

Wet bulb temperature

The **temperature** recorded by a **thermometer** whose bulb is wrapped in a wet material. The purpose of this is to find out how quickly **evaporation** is taking place. As evaporation occurs, it takes heat from the thermometer bulb, and the thermometer reads a lower value. When the air is saturated, no **evaporation** takes place, and the ordinary (dry bulb) and wet bulb thermometers read the same.

Measurements from wet and dry bulb thermometers allow the calculation of relative **humidity**.

Whirlwind

A violently spiraling column of air similar to, but smaller than, a **tornado**. Whirlwinds have many regional names, including **dust devil** and willy willy.

White out

A condition in which the sky is overcast, and a **blizzard** is blowing, so that it is impossible to see any horizon or anything more than a few meters away.

Wind

The flow of air across the surface of the Earth. It is measured in terms of speed (by an **anemometer**) and direction (by a **wind vane**). (*See:* **Beaufort scale** and **Windsock**.)

Winds occur because of changes in air **temperature** and **pressure**.

Changes of temperature cause local winds, such as **thermals** and **sea breezes**. The global **circulation** of the **atmosphere** is also caused by differences in temperature between the hot equator and the cold poles. As air flows from the equator to the poles, it is caught by the rotation of the Earth, and its direction is changed. Winds flowing to the poles move in a northeasterly direction in the Northern Hemisphere (and so are called southwesterly winds) and in a southeasterly direction in the Southern Hemisphere (and so are called northwesterly winds).

Return flows of air produce winds in the opposite directions. The northeasterly and southeasterly winds are called the **trade winds**.

Winds also occur when a **low-pressure** region and **high-pressure** region are close together. Air spirals down and out of a high-pressure region and up and into a low-pressure region. Buy's Ballots Law uses the wind to tell where the pressure systems are. If you stand in the Northern Hemisphere with your back to the wind, the low pressure is on your left-hand side. In the Southern Hemisphere the reverse is true.

(*For types of wind see*: **Bora**; **Buster**; **Chinook**; **Doctor**; **Downdraft**; **Friagem**; **Haboob**; **Harmattan**; **Khamsin**; **Mistral**; **Monsoon**; **Northeaster, noreaster**; **Norther**; **Pampero**; **Santa Ana**; **Simoom**; **Sirocco**; **Trade winds**.)

Wind chill

This is the combined effect of air **temperature** and **wind** that produces a "biting wind." We are all familiar with the cooling effect of a summer **breeze**. The flow of air over the skin carries away perspiration and makes the skin cooler. The same combined effect of temperature and wind in cold conditions is called wind chill, and it can cause people to lose heat from their skin faster than their bodies can replace it. In severe cases the effects of wind chill can be life-threatening. This most often happens to mountain climbers and others in exposed places during winter.

Windsock

A conical instrument used to measure **wind** speed and direction.

Wind vane

An instrument, often shaped like an arrow, that swivels to show **wind** direction.

▼ **Wind**—Strong prevailing winds may make it impossible for trees to grow up straight. Trees like this are therefore a useful indicator of the exposure of a site to winds.

▼ **Windsock**

Windward

The coast or flank of a mountain facing the prevailing **winds**. Windward coasts not only have frequent strong winds, but also, as the air is forced to rise over the land, it cools and releases its **moisture** as **cloud** and **rain**. As a result, windward areas usually get plentiful rain. Relief effects (*see:* **Orographic effect**) from windward areas are important to both the **trade winds** and the **midlatitude westerlies**.

Index